DETERMINI

DESPERATE

"Developing a deep-seated desperation for Jesus Christ"

By: Josh Howard

Hoffman and Co. Publishing

HoffmanCoPublishing.com

You need to be desperate for Jesus Christ. If there is anywhere else that you feel you can go besides Jesus, you need to come to an understanding of just how lost and hopeless you are without Him. For the Christian this walk is impossible without a desperation for the Savior. For the lost hell is the only destination without a desperation for Jesus Christ. You need to be desperate for Jesus, and that kind of desperation doesn't happen by accident. We don't live in a culture that wants to be desperate. We live in a world that will tell you to get up and trudge on. Be strong. Move forward. Be all you want to be and lean on nobody but yourself. But that is not what scripture calls us to.

There is a life that is abundant. There is a love that is free and freeing at the same time. There is a savior who desperately loves you when you least deserve it and wants to transform you. All you need is a desperation for Him. The more desperate that you become for Jesus, the more that you cast away of yourself in exchange for Him, the more you will be able to live. You need to be desperate for Jesus, and it is my prayer that this book will help you flesh out that determination. As you read "Determined to be Desperate" I hope that you will read it prayerfully and take everything I say back to scripture. The word of the Lord is infallible, I am not. I hope that you will pray for the Lord of Armies to reveal Himself to you as you read. I hope that you will take an honest and prayerful look into the depths of your own broken heart and allow Jesus Christ to lead you ever deeper into a desperation for Him. As you read this book be in prayer, and know that I am praying for you as you read as I have determined to pray over every person who picks up a copy of this book, known or unknown by me. I pray this book is a blessing and a humble exhortation, and aids in leading you to a deeper love of the One who took on flesh to set you free for eternity.

Determine to be desperate.

"By a matchless parable our Lord there taught us that all believers are branches of the Living Vine, and that, apart from Him we are nothing and can do nothing because we have in us no life."

* A.T Pierson

What are you desperate for? Seriously, what is it that you dream about at night? Chances are something just popped into your head because, face it, night and day you can't stop thinking about it. Maybe it's that scholarship that you so desperately need because there is no way you can afford that college. Or maybe you're chasing that perfect reflection. As soon as you get home from work or school you just can't wait to hit the weight room and pound your muscles for a solid hour but, be honest, you know you will never be satisfied with what stares back at you from that glass. Maybe you immediately thought of financial stability.

Are you a workaholic? Do you rise earlier than anyone else, and stay up late into the night chasing that next promotion? Whether it is what you think others desire of you, or a dream that you need to achieve for yourself, you are desperate for something. You can't help it. You were made that way. There is a hole in your heart, and it needs to be filled. When sin entered the world, your heart was burdened with the need for Jesus Christ. Jesus identified this need in the first line of the most famous sermon ever given, the Sermon on the Mount, when He said, *"Blessed are the poor in spirit, for theirs is the kingdom of heaven."*

The problem is that we are human, and we seek the things of this world to try to fill this hole. If you have never accepted the grace and mercy that only the Son of God can offer, and you happened to pick up this book by accident, good! This is exactly where you need to be right now because, unless you become poor in spirit (we will address exactly what that means later on) there is no chance for salvation.

However; if you have accepted Jesus Christ as your Lord and Savior, don't check out! You don't get a pass on this one either because desperation for Jesus Christ isn't a "one and done" sort of thing. No, you must daily be poor in spirit, desperately seeking the heart of the one true Savior, or your walk will surely fall painfully short of the calling placed on your life at the moment of your salvation. As you read this book, pray. Ask the Lord to impart on you a heart that is poor in spirit, and a determination to be desperate for Jesus Christ.

"THE UPWARD LOOK"

"I gave in, and admitted that God was God"

* *C.S. Lewis*

It would be impossible to become desperate for Jesus Christ without first seeing God. I love the story of the call of Isaiah because Isaiah gets a pretty eye-opening rundown of how the Christian walk is meant to look. I mean, if there is one prophet who undoubtedly predicted the coming of Jesus Christ, and the

salvation that would come with Him, it was Isaiah.

The name Isaiah itself, in Hebrew, means "Yahweh

saves!" That's why, for the first part of this book, we

are going to take a serious look at the moment that

Isaiah became desperate for Jesus Christ.

Picture this…

You're sitting at the dinner table having a nice meal

with your family. Or maybe you just sat down in front

of the T.V after a long day at work. Or maybe you're

sitting right where you are now, reading a

phenomenal book (ahem!), when you see God! I'm not talking about a picture of God, or even an epiphany about a scripture you read earlier. I'm talking about God. The Lord of hosts, the Holy of Holies, the creator of heaven and earth…. That's exactly what happened to Isaiah. He doesn't write what he was doing, or where he was, Isaiah simply tells us that in the year that King Uzziah died,

"I saw the Lord seated on a high and lofty throne, and His robe filled the temple. Seraphim were standing above Him; each one had six wings: with two he covered his face, with two he covered his feet, and with two he flew. And one called to another:

Holy, holy, holy is the Lord of Armies; His glory fills

the whole earth.

The foundations of the doorways shook at the sound

of their voices, and the temple was filled with smoke."

Can you imagine? What a way to get a firsthand understanding of exactly who God is! As Isaiah looked up from whatever he was doing, the scene that unfolded above him must have been astonishing! In an instant he was transported to the throne room of heaven, and there sat God. If you're not feeling overwhelmed right now, go back and read the scripture above and let yourself imagine being cast into that moment. There sits God, on the throne of heaven, and this is no ordinary throne. No one on this earth has ever seen a throne like what Isaiah must have beheld in that moment. In Revelation John gives us a glimpse of what Isaiah may have seen when he looked at the throne of God, and it's still unimaginable. John tells us that the throne on which the God of heaven and earth sits is surrounded by a rainbow that looks like an emerald. He writes that flashes of lightning shoot forth from the throne of God, and rumblings of thunder roll out from it. Seven fiery torches burn night and day around the throne, and something like a sea of glass stretches out before it as far as the eye can see. Isaiah writes that the throne on which the Lord sat was "high and lofty."

Imagine what it takes for the throne of heaven to sit

high above the infinite throne room of heaven. We

don't get a description of the vastness of the throne

room, except that it is the throne room of heaven! We

must imagine that the mighty throne room of heaven

stretches infinitely outward, and infinitely upward,

and the throne of God sits high and lifted up above

the throne room. This isn't a throne that any man can

sit on. This is a throne built to seat the Ruler of

heaven and earth. This is THE throne. And that's just

what the finite words of this world are able to

describe! There is no way that we can even begin to

imagine the majesty of the throne that stood before Isaiah as he looked up into the throne room of heaven.

But that's not all. As awesome and breathtaking as the throne of heaven must have been in this moment, it pales in comparison to the one who sat on it. Isaiah writes that the robe of God filled the temple in which He sat. Again, we must imagine the vastness of the throne room of heaven, infinite in scale, and the robe of God billows forth and fills the infinite temple of heaven. Our minds cannot even begin to comprehend it, and the longer you sit and try to imagine it the harder it is to grasp. And this is what fills the vision of Isaiah in the year that king Uzziah died.

I don't want to skip over the train of the robe of God, because the beauty and magnitude of every detail of Isaiah's vision in chapter six is vital to our understanding of who God is. The train of God's robe represents the power of the Almighty. In the time of Isaiah, when a king conquered another king, he would behead that king and cut off the train of his robe, attaching it to the train of his own. The length of a king's train was used to illustrate his power, how many, and the identity of the other kings that he had conquered. That alone gives a whole new meaning to the name King of kings. There is no king who does not fall under the reign of Yahweh, the God of the Bible. There is no power that can compare to the power of the Lord of hosts. And Isaiah stood, in that moment, in the presence of the infinite power of God.

But the train of God's robe is only a portion of what Isaiah beheld in the throne room of the Lord. When John found himself in the same room, looking at the Lord on His throne, he said that God looked like Jasper and Carnelian stone. In biblical times jasper is described as being clear, like crystal, and carnelian was a fiery red stone. The one seated on the throne in

Revelation 4 would have shone like the brightest sun. It's no wonder John doesn't look upon the Lord long before he falls to his face in utter fear!

Back in Isaiah's vision we not only see the throne of heaven, and the One who sits on it, but the wonder of what is happening around the throne of God. Around the throne of God were seraphim, and these weren't baby-faced angels with harps and diapers. The word *seraphim* in Hebrew means "burning one." These guys were on fire, and they were magnificent. The seraphim are beings that would make even the strongest man fall on his face with fear and trembling, and they dwell in the throne room for the sole purpose

of serving God. Isaiah writes that each of the

seraphim had six wings, and that each pair of wings

had a specific purpose. With two wings each seraph

covered his eyes, a gesture that shows that, as

magnificent as the seraphim are, they are not worthy

to look upon the God of heaven. Imagine being in

Isaiah's place, eyes upon God, and even the burning

angels around Him aren't worthy to set their eyes

upon Him!

Not only were the seraphim covering their eyes, but

they covered their feet as well with the second pair of

wings. The seraphim, magnificent angels that hovered around the throne in service to God, remained forever in humility before the Lord. In the time of Isaiah, shoes weren't a reality quite yet. As a result, your feet got pretty dirty. The angels of heaven covered their lowliest parts in humility before the Lord. It was an act of extreme reverence. The feet are a common symbol of humility throughout scripture. When Jesus enters the scene in Mark 1, John the Baptist exclaims that he is not even worthy to bend and unstrap the sandal on the feet of Jesus. In Luke we find the woman, a sinner, bowing before Jesus and washing his feet with her hair. The thought of even touching a man's feet would have been repulsive to anyone in that time, and yet this woman found the desperate need to humble herself and, as well as she could, wash the feet of the one who would take the punishment for all of her sin. How powerful the God of heaven must be if the burning angels around His throne feel the need to express their utmost humility before Him.

The final set of wings that each seraph possesses are simply used to serve. *"With two they flew"* shows us that the seraphim were ready to do the bidding of the Lord at His command. The magnificent burning ones who surround the throne of Heaven are constantly ready to do the will of the one who sits on the throne, and this is seen all throughout scripture. David wrote about angels in the Psalms, that they are mighty in strength, and that they do the Lord's bidding and obey the voice of His Word. An angel came to Jesus in the wilderness to minister to Him, and showed up later in the garden to minister once again as Jesus prayed before His crucifixion. There is not an angel in Heaven who is not bound to the will of God!

As amazing as it must have been to see the seraphim flying around the throne of God, expressing their unworthiness to even be in His presence and

performing His every will, what is even more

awesome is the worship that Isaiah got the chance to

experience. Even as the Seraphim flew from place to

place, covering their feet and eyes, they were crying

out eternally, *"Holy, holy, holy is the Lord of Armies;*

His glory fills the whole earth." I mean, imagine

receiving that glimpse of heaven. This was far more

than just a worship service; this worship is eternal.

From eternity to eternity the God of heavens has been

worshipped. From beginning to end the Lord has been

worthy to be worshipped. Can you grasp that? I mean

really grasp it. We worship, or if you are reading this

as a non-believer, you have seen people worship. We go to and from church every week and we may even pour out our hearts before God in a truly moving worship service. But the worship in heaven does not end. I have cried while worshipping the Lord. I have laughed, clapped, jumped for joy, prayed, and gotten on my knees in worship to God. But I can't even begin to imagine the beauty of what Isaiah witnessed in this moment. Can you wait to get to heaven to see this kind of worship? Can you even stand to wait another moment to stand in awe of the one who is worthy to be worshipped from eternity to eternity?

Because that's what desperation is all about.

If you can read the account of Isaiah's encounter with

God, and not squirm in angst to be with the One who

sits on that throne, then you desperately need to

encounter God in a real way. You need a proper view

of God, the God of heaven and earth, the One who

spoke everything into existence. You have a deep

need to see that God is holy, that He cannot dwell

amongst your sin, and that you are deserving of

nothing short of death in His presence. You need an

"Oh" moment.

I grew up in church. I have heard my whole life about how great God is. I've read stories of His majesty all through my life and learned of His holiness throughout my entire childhood. My head knowledge about God was stacked by the time I was twenty years old. But I needed an "Oh" moment. When I turned twenty, I didn't have a solid heart knowledge of God. I had been a decent kid my whole life, and I had kept the commandments pretty well, but my heart had not come to a full knowledge of who God was, and my world was about to be rocked. Just like the rich young ruler, I thought I was doing pretty well. But the way that God showed me just how powerful He is was an earth shaker for me. From the outside of my heart, looking in, nobody would have really noticed, but I did. The Lord got ahold of my heart. He pulled back the veil and said, "here I AM". And from that time, I will never be the same. I have been given a strong desire to know Jesus more every day rather than just following a set of rules that can never change me.

Isaiah was called to prophesy the coming of the Savior years before Jesus would even appear; but, in order to do that, Isaiah needed to experience the salvation about which he was going to be preaching. Isaiah needed to become desperate for Jesus Christ, and so do you.

You are reading this book for a reason. Hopefully you picked this book up because you have a deep desire to be desperate for Jesus. Maybe you had that desperation in the past, but it has faded, and you feel lost. Or maybe you have been saved for years but you have never truly felt a desperation for Jesus. In other words, your relationship with Christ has yet to move from your head to your heart. Even if you have never accepted Jesus Christ as your savior, your desperation must begin with God. You need to see just how magnificent and holy the God of the universe is, and only He can show that to you. This book will never do justice to the glory of God. I could write a million pages and not even begin to scratch the surface of who God is, and that is why you need to pray. So stop, right now, stop and pray that God will show Himself to you. I urge you to call out to the Lord as you continue to read this book, and before reading on, to ask Him to reveal Himself to you.

And once you have…

Let me tell you just how magnificent God is.

"ETERNAL GLORY"

The entirety of scripture speaks to the glory of God. It begins with His glory, *"In the beginning God…"* and it ends with His glory, *"He who testifies about thee sayings says, "yes I am coming soon". Amen! Come Lord Jesus! The grace of the Lord Jesus be with everyone. Amen."* Every word, from the beginning of scripture, to the end, testifies of the glory of God. But scripture is not the only place that we find the glory of God. No, all of creation shouts that God is holy. From the beautiful rising of the sun, to its majestic setting, everything speaks of God's glory. Do you remember when you were saved? If you do, then you remember the newness of life. You remember that everything had a new magnificence to it. You may not have understood how the bird remains in the air, but you knew it was because of God. You might not have fully understood the rivers and the mountains, and how all of this wonderful creation continues to thrive, but you knew it was of God. And it was glorious to you! That's the God that your heart is hungering for. That is the God that your soul needs. I mean, you picked up a book titled, "Determined to be Desperate." Nobody wants to be desperate, unless they have felt their need for the God of the universe. David had this kind of need for God. The greatest king of Israel could not peel himself away from his wonder of the Lord Almighty. That's what the Psalms are all about! Psalm 93 proclaims, *"Your throne has been established from the beginning, you are from eternity."* David goes on to say that even the floods praise God. Imagine that. We have seen the disaster that a flood can bring. There is no one on earth who can stand against a mighty flood and bring it to a stop, that man would be obliterated the moment the waters hit him. But even the floods praise the name of God and listen to His voice! From before the beginning of this world God has been in absolute control. He has lived in holiness from eternity to eternity. He cannot be slowed down even by the most powerful of rulers, and he cannot be controlled by even the strongest of angels. There are so many scriptures that speak to the glory of God, I could fill this entire book simply with scripture, and never reach the magnitude of who God is. But God's majesty is not just a story we read about in scripture. It is all around you, and you are in desperate need of a reminder of just who God is.

As I sat down to write this book, I began to pray that God would reveal Himself to me. Like Isaiah, I have no place writing about something that I have not experienced myself, and though I have seen the glory of God throughout my life, I needed a fresh reminder. So, I prayed…and I prayed. And then I prayed some more. I became frustrated with God because I just needed a sign. I needed to know how powerful He was, and I thought that He wasn't giving it to me. It would be so much easier to write about God's glory if he would just crack the sky a little bit, right? But then I began to stop talking to God, and start listening for Him, and He showed me. I started to think about eternity. I started to dwell on heaven. How it never began, and it will never end. I thought for days on the fact that God has no beginning, and that there was nothing before Him, not even time! And, to be honest, it made my head spin. The longer I tried to unravel all of who God is, the more confused I got. Then it hit me. That was my sign! I had looked for days for a crack in the sky, a glimpse of His face somewhere, an angel to come in a dream and show God to me, and I neglected to simply THINK on God. The Lord took me back to His word, and reminded me of Colossians 3, *"So if you have been raised with Christ, seek the things above, where Christ is, seated at the right hand of God. Set your mind on things above, not on earthly things."* I realized that looking for God is absolutely acceptable, but we ought not to look for Him to bring some special sign, but we should look to where He already is. That is, God has already revealed Himself time and time again. The glory of God is all around us, in scripture, in creation, and in the depths of our own hearts. God is so powerful that there is no one on earth who doesn't sense His glory, we are all made in His image after all. God has done things in your life that are unimaginable. He has shown himself to you repeatedly, and sometimes it's simply a matter of stopping for a few moments and allowing Him to remind you of these things. Be like David. Pray that the Lord would search you, that He would show you Himself in your own heart. And this prayer isn't only for the believer! If you happen to be reading this, and you don't know Jesus Christ, Praise God! He will still

reveal Himself to you if you ask, in fact, He already

has. You simply need to see it. So, I want you to stop

again. I pray you don't read on past this point until

you have. Remember that this book is not simply

meant to be read, put aside, and talked about from

time to time. This book is meant to be prayed through.

This book is written to bring you back to scripture,

and lead you to think on heavenly things, and I hope

that is what you will do before you move on to the

next chapter because, if you don't, you will be turned

off by what it has to say.

See, the next step in developing a desperation for Jesus is the toughest part of the whole process. The inescapable result of seeing the glory of God is understanding just how broken you are in His presence. And that is going to hurt...a lot.

So please pray. Pray that God will show you His heart, so that you can come to grips with your own. Pray that God will reveal to you his holiness, so that you will see that you have none. Pray that the Lord who can, will lead you to pray as Isaiah did, *"woe is me, for I am undone."*

Because you need to experience the glory of God, the opposite nature that resides in you, and the grace that Jesus brings to bridge that gap, before you can ever become desperate for Him.

"THE INWARD LOOK"

"Shallow are the souls that have forgotten how to

shudder"

* Leon Kass

You know you are broken.

Even if no other soul on the planet sees it, you know

it to be true. You are messed up, and no one feels that

more than you do. You are stuck in the cycle, the

same cycle Paul found himself stuck in. You are

constantly doing the things you don't want to do and,

no matter how hard you try, you can't possibly make

yourself do the things you want to do. Every day you

find yourself looking in the mirror asking, *"Why are*

you like this?"

The answer?

You are full of sin. From the tips of your toes, to the

very top of your head, you are sick. And you know it.

But as aware of your own shortcomings as you may

have been before, if you took the previous chapter

seriously and prayerfully, you are infinitely more aware of them now. When you come to grips with exactly who the God of the universe is the only thing you will be able to see is just how short you fall of His perfect holiness. This is where we find Isaiah in verse five of chapter six. Isaiah has just looked up into the throne room of heaven. He has stood before the holy God of the universe, seen His majesty, witnessed that even the angels are unworthy to look upon Him, and has been left in the pit of his own sin. In verse five Isaiah exclaims *"Woe is me for I am ruined because I am a man of unclean lips and live among a people of unclean lips, and because my eyes have seen the King, the Lord of Armies."* The short

version of that is, "I am a dead man." Isaiah knew that

he had come face to face with the God of the

universe, the God who stands holy and pure above all

else, and Isaiah knew that he was sinful. What do you

do in that moment? Isaiah knew that the only option

was his own death. The bible says that no one can

look on God and live. No one can stand in the

presence of the almighty and walk away, because the

sin in each of our hearts is only worthy of justice,

justice that must come by death. It is difficult for us to

understand the sheer terror in Isaiah's words as we

read this passage of scripture. The Bible doesn't say

whether Isaiah fell upon his face or not, but I am more than willing to imagine that he did. Afterall; he knew that the full wrath of God was just about to rain down upon him, and I don't think that I would be too excited to see that coming down on me.

Beyond the setting that Isaiah finds himself in, the language with which he expresses his suffering in this moment is telling of just how helpless he was feeling. As Isaiah looks up and sees the Lord high and lifted up, seated on His throne in heaven, he exclaims *"Woe is me for I am ruined!"* Woe was most often reserved for the wicked throughout the old testament. Jeremiah expresses the same sentiment as he preaches the coming wrath of God on Jerusalem, *"Look He advances like clouds; His chariots are like a storm. His horses are swifter than eagles, woe to us for we are ruined!"* By expressing woe upon himself, Isaiah is proclaiming his own wickedness in the presence of God, and the deepest sense of dread that the human heart can express. The disconnect that we tend to feel with this passage of scripture is that we have lost our sense of woe. No one would shout "woe is me" today, it's simply not the way we talk, so it is quite easy to read over this short line in Isaiah's exclamation and forget about it completely. But we have a desperate need to understand what Isaiah was feeling in the presence of the Most High God. Imagine driving your car down the street one afternoon. You pull up to a stop sign and, without even thinking, you pull right on through. You've stopped at this stop sign hundreds of times. It's a slow intersection, and you almost never have to wait to pull through. In fact, if your honest, you usually pull a rolling stop at this intersection. But this time is different. This time, as you pull into the center of the intersection, a semi horn blows. You look up to your left and there it is, the front of a monstrous semi-truck is right on top of you, and there is nothing left to be done. Now stop that moment. Can you feel it? The sense of woe would be massive in this instant. You know you are going to die, and there is nothing that you can do about it. Every decision you made today, up to this fatal point, flashes through your mind in an instant and you know that it is over. You can't speak. You can't even shout. You will never be able to tell the semi driver that you are sorry or explain to your family why you did what you did, it's just over without a word.

This is the way Isaiah must have felt in the presence of God. He knew that his time was over and, worse yet, he knew it was completely his doing. There was nothing he could say to the God of Armies. There was no defense that he could give to the Lord as he stood at the foot of the throne of judgement. Isaiah knew it was over. I want to stop in this moment and spend so much time on it because we all need to have this moment. This single moment is paramount in the life of the Christian. If you are ever to be desperate for Jesus Christ, you need to feel the depth of your inadequacy before the Lord. If you have never felt helpless before the Lord, you have never truly known a need for Jesus Christ.

As I said in the first chapter, I lived a large portion of my Christian walk this way. I knew I was a sinner. I knew that I needed Jesus to save me, but I had never stood face to face with God, staring into the filthiness of my heart. As a result, my faith became based on the boxes that I could check off. Sure, I had a crippling porn addiction until well after I was out of high school, but I didn't smoke weed. Yes, I cursed here and there, but I had never had a drop of alcohol. Of course, I told lies when I wanted to stay out of trouble, but I wore my purity ring and was saving myself for marriage. This was my idea of the Christian walk. I allowed myself to believe that if my sins were kept out of sight from the world, that I was doing well, but this led to many deeper issues. As I struggled into the end of my teen years my presumed righteousness began to take its toll on me. I wasn't leaning on Christ, but on what I could do. I wasn't desperate for Jesus I was just desperate to keep a good reputation. Because I leaned on my own strength and understanding, all of those boxes I had checked throughout my walk with Christ began to be un-checked. At nineteen years old I dove headfirst into alcoholism. Because I peeled back my inhibitions with alcohol, I gave away the one thing that I held most dear to my heart; my desire to save myself for my future wife. I spent the better part of nineteen years old clutched in the grips of my sin, because I wasn't desperate for the one who freed me from sin. I had become so convinced of my own goodness, that I completely neglected the one who died to impart His goodness on me, and the life I was living wore me down quickly. I remember my "oh" moment vividly. I didn't have a vision in the way that Isaiah did, but I saw who my God was nonetheless. As I laid in my bed the night after my twentieth birthday I couldn't sleep. I didn't feel like I could pray. I was on the verge of walking away from the Lord because I didn't feel like He could ever have me back. I had known His commands my whole life and broken them anyways. I wouldn't have wasted my time on me, but the spirit began to pray on my behalf. I remember laying in my bed and simply praying, *"God, change my heart or let me go, because I can't keep doing this."* And He heard me, He had always heard me. God hadn't walked away from me, He was simply waiting for me to be ready to see the depths of my filthy heart, and it was in that moment that He began to work a mighty change within my heart.

This is what Isaiah saw when He stood in front of the Lord of Hosts. In this moment he was so vividly aware of the filthiness of his own heart that he couldn't say a word. The exclamation, *"I am ruined!"*

is summed up in the Hebrew word, *"damah."* It means *"I must be silent",* or *"I must perish."* Isaiah was saying that he had no defense in the presence of God. The only outcome he saw was his own immediate death, and it caused him to call down woe upon himself. Have you come to that view of yourself? Can you remember a moment, or many moments if you're as stubborn as I am, when you were faced with an honest view of your own wretchedness? God *wants* you to see it, because you desperately need to see it. Jesus, in His first sermon we are given in scripture, the Sermon on the Mount, began by saying, *"blessed are the poor in spirit, for theirs is the kingdom of heaven."* That idea of being

poor in spirit is anything but light-hearted. In order to

become poor in spirit we need to come to the

understanding that we, of our own power, have

nothing to bring to the table of the Most High God.

We need to understand that our own righteousness is

nothing more than filthy rags, useless and messy. But

in the hands of the Lord our filthy rags are made new.

But there is also a flip side to this particular beatitude.

If the poor in spirit will inherit the kingdom of

heaven, then those who never become poor in spirit

can never enter into the kingdom of heaven. In short,

if you are never made aware of your own dire

shortcomings, you will never be able to walk in the

saving grace of Jesus Christ.

You need to be broken by your own sinfulness. You don't need to become bogged down in it. You don't need to wallow in it or return to it like a dog to its vomit. But you need to be broken over your sin the way God is broken over your sin. The reality of being human is that your sin was enough to keep you from a holy and loving God for all of eternity. Your sin was so dire that the son of God had to come down from heaven, live a sinless life, die on a cross, and rise again to give you any way to be made right with God.

You held the nails that pierced His hands and feet. You cried out from the crowd, *"Crucify Him!"* It was your sin that made it necessary for the God of the universe to die. And you need to know that.

David was stellar at this. David was a man who, though he was considered a man after God's heart, was deeply broken, and nobody knew it better than him. David probably spent more time in repentance before God than he spent doing anything else… because he was constantly in need of it. I love to read the Psalms because David had a way of putting the depths of his heart down on paper. In Psalm 38 David comes before the Lord exclaiming, *"There is no soundness in my body because of your indignation; there is no health in my bones because of my sin. For my iniquities have flooded over my head; they are a burden too heavy for me to bear. My wounds are foul and festering because of my foolishness."* And he goes on! David continues to say that he is bent over because of his mourning, and that he groans because of the anguish in his heart over his own sin. Psalm 51 is a plea to God for restoration after his adultery with Bathsheba and murder of Uriah, her husband. David refers to his life as dust in Psalm 119 and begs God to show him the depths of the sin in his heart in Psalm

139. I could go on for an entire book on David's awareness of his own sin. I think that this was the main reason that David was called a man after God's own heart. It wasn't because he was perfect, quite obviously, but because he was literally *after* the heart of God. David was constantly chasing the heart of God. He longed for it day and night and he never ceased in falling on his face before the Most High God.

But this isn't nearly as easy as it may sound. Strictly from a human nature standpoint, we don't like to feel like we are broken. Nobody wants to admit that we cannot get through on our own. I mean what kind of weak person can't pick themselves up and move on down the road right? So, we refuse to admit our own brokenness and no one ever will, apart from a real encounter with the God of Armies. That is why we must constantly come back to each of these steps.

Understanding who God is isn't something that happens once in the life of the desperate Christian. It needs to be constant. You need to be constantly revisiting the God of the Bible so that you may have a true understanding of who you are. We don't decide that we are broken on our own, it must begin with God.

Culture will never show you how broken you are. We live in a culture that tells you that you're good to go as long as you're happy, so why is our culture unhappier than it has ever been? We have already established that you will never sufficiently admit, on your own, how broken you are. It hurts to admit that we're messed up and your human nature will never allow you to do that on your own. Self-help books, motivational speakers, world influencers, will always begin with the idea that there is a goodness inside of you that simply needs to be released. As a result, we feel like we can earn love. Love from others. Love from ourselves. Love from whatever god you choose to believe in. It's all based on whether or not you live up to your potential. And that is what leaves people hollow and depressed. The truth is that you have no potential apart from Jesus Christ. You could work a thousand lifetimes and never measure up. It's why you struggle to feel good enough, because you know that you're not. It's why you often feel like, even when you do something right, you're always wrong.

It's because that is the state of your flesh, always wrong. And God wants to show you that in a way that hurts so deeply that His mercy leaves you awe-struck. That's right, you're going to have to hurt to be made whole, but the hurt of admitting your own brokenness will lead to the most fulfilling life you couldn't even

begin to imagine living.

So, what does it look like to admit that you're

broken? Do you need to rip your clothes in anguish,

pour dust over your head, and walk around in sack-

cloths for the next few days? If that's what it takes,

absolutely! But it probably won't look like that for

you or me. But I promise that it will be just as world

rocking as some of the Old Testament customs sound.

The first thing you need to do is mourn. You're

broken! You have messed up royally. And you have murdered the Son of God! That's right. It was your sin that held Christ to the cross. It was your sin that yelled *"Crucify Him!"* from the crowd. It was your sin that betrayed the King of kings for thirty pieces of silver. And it was my sin, and the sin of every individual person throughout this world, and that is something to mourn over. Isaiah's exclamation of *"Woe is me!"* was far more than mere sentiment. It was a cry of anguish. I imagine that Isaiah felt physical pain over his own brokenness. Much like the pit that you will get in your stomach when you have to apologize to someone whom you have hurt deeply,

Isaiah stood in front of the Almighty God, whom he had hurt deeply. And it pained him. It caused him woe. It led him to mourn over his own brokenness. And it ushered him into repentance. You will never come to God's understanding of how messed up you are without feeling the need to mourn. James tells us to *"be miserable and mourn and weep. Let your laughter be turned to mourning and your joy to gloom. Humble yourselves before the Lord and He will exalt you."* He is speaking to sinners! He is speaking to you. That doesn't mean that God wants you to live in a constant state of sadness, but it does mean that you desperately need to be broken in order to experience the joy that only Jesus Christ can bring.

So mourn! Mourn loudly. Mourn openly before God.

Lament your own brokenness. Cry out to God,

humble yourself before the Lord of Armies, and be

broken over your brokenness. You will never know

true joy until you do.

Once you have come to a place of absolute

brokenness over your own sin, you need to confess

your sin to God. I know what you're thinking, *"God

knows my sin, what good will it do me to tell Him

what He already knows?"* The answer? It will do a

world of good! You need to confess your sin to God.

Confess specifically and confess out loud. That's exactly what Isaiah did after he mourned over his own brokenness. After he called down woe on himself, and exclaimed that he was ruined, Isaiah began to confess his sin out loud to the Lord, *"I am a man of unclean lips and live among a people of unclean lips…"* That's right, Isaiah confessed that he was a potty mouth. The man who had just preached for five whole chapters is confessing to God that his own lips are filthy. Notice how specific Isaiah is as he bares his sins before God. As you begin to confess your sin you need to confess it specifically. David asked God to show him any unclean way that was in his own heart.

Nehemiah confesses very similarly to God in the first chapter of his book. (Notice that he also begins with mourning) Job exclaims that he is just dust and ashes in the presence of God as he repents for questioning the Lord. You must exercise in confessing your sin, by name, before the Lord. God doesn't need to hear it, He already knows. But you do. You need to hear your sin come out of your mouth. You need to hear your brokenness named. And you need to be the one to name it. That is why, on top of confessing specifically, you need to confess out loud. You have a desperate need to taste the filth of your sin as it leaves your lips. You must understand the awful feeling of speaking your shortcomings out loud.

Yes, it's going to hurt.

It will be terribly difficult to say those words, and it never gets any easier. Every time I confess my sins out loud it makes me shudder. As I admit to God, and myself, the acts that I despise within my heart I find my voice weak and shaky. And that's a good thing! It means that I am still convicted by my sin. It means that I am disgusted by my own wickedness. And you need to reach that point.

Sure, sometimes it is beneficial to confess to God quietly. When you are convicted you have a need to confess immediately, and sometimes, yelling out your sin just isn't appropriate. But if you able, lift up your sin to God audibly. It isn't difficult to confess in your head. I find it quite easy sometimes to bow my head and think a quick confession. *"God, please forgive me for my sin, Amen."* We do this all the time, and it's not bad in and of itself. But desperation requires a little more investment. Jesus forgave you of your sin two thousand years ago when He died on a cross and rose again from death. But the Holy Spirit still needs to do some work in you in order for you to find yourself desperate for Jesus Christ and a large part of that work is breaking your heart over the state of your heart. Set aside some time (and probably some Kleenex) to confess your sins, specifically and audibly, to God. I guarantee you that He will do a work in you and begin to lead you into a desperation for Jesus like you have never experienced before.

Before the final point in admitting that you are broken, I want to touch on something that we see the prophet Isaiah do, as well as Nehemiah and many other biblical characters who found themselves desperate for the coming salvation.

They confessed the sins of the people. I know, it sounds crazy. Who are you to bring someone else's sin before God, right? But this seems to be an important step in the lives of people who lived out a desperation for the Lord. We will dive deeper into this idea in a later chapter, but the key concept here is that your brokenness over your own sin *will* lead to a brokenness over the sin around you. As you realize your desperate need for Jesus Christ, you will feel, more deeply, the desperate need that every lost person has for that very same Jesus. Never neglect to come before the Lord in intercession (praying for others) as you come before Him in supplication (praying for yourself), even in confessing sin. Pray for your

nation, your family, your friends, and your enemies,

as you come before the God of all.

Finally, as you seek to be broken over your own

sinfulness before God, come back to God! Isaiah

exclaims his woe, confesses his sins as well as the

sins of his nation, and then again expresses the

majesty of the God in front of whom he stands. As

you are made woefully aware of your own sin make

sure not to lose your vision of just who God is. It will

be terrifying, it will be difficult, and it will be

overwhelming, but you must remember that God is

holy. As you come to grips with your own brokenness, allow God to make you ever more aware of Him. And praise Him in the midst of the breaking. Tell Him how awesome He is. Exclaim to Him how powerful and holy He is. Tell Him how wonderful He is. Praise Him through the breaking as Isaiah did, as Nehemiah did, and as David so often did. Even as He breaks your heart, God is worthy to be praised.

You need to become poor in spirit to inherit the kingdom of heaven. You must be made low to be lifted up. You desperately need to be broken in order to be made whole. The deliberate determination to be poor in spirit means that you will need to visit, often,

the fact that you have nothing to bring to the table of

the Most High God. Because, once you have admitted

that, confessed your brokenness, and humbled

yourself before God, only then can you experience the

marvelous grace and mercy of our Lord Jesus Christ!

[Stop here a moment. I urge you to stop and pray

before you read further. If you have not confessed

your sin, specifically and audibly, before God I urge

you to do so before continuing on. Please pray as you

move to the next chapter of this book and, if you have

never accepted Jesus Christ as the Lord and Savior of

your life, prepare your heart to meet Him face to face,

because the next glorious step in becoming desperate

for Jesus is receiving Him.]

"BEHOLD THE LAMB!"

"For nothing counts with God, except His beloved son, Jesus Christ, who is completely pure and holy before Him. Where He is, there God looks and has His pleasure."

* Martin Luther

It's all about Jesus.

From the first letter of Genesis, to the final word of Revelation, It's all about Jesus Christ. The Old

Testament points to the coming of Jesus Christ, and the New Testament reveals the promise that was made so many years before Christ ever walked the earth. You must realize, Jesus wasn't plan B. He was the plan from the beginning… the Son of God given for your sin. When John the Baptist first saw the savior that he had preached about for so long he cried out, *"Here is the Lamb of God, who takes away the sin of the world!"* All of John chapter 1 reveals that Jesus was there in the very beginning with God, and that He knew from the beginning what He would have to do to restore mankind to God. To restore *you* to God. Even the very beginning, the story of creation, shows that the death, burial, and resurrection of Jesus was always the plan. In the midst of the creation of the world God proclaimed, *"let US create man in our own image."* It's no accident that this part of creation was written into scripture. John tells us that Jesus was there at the creation of the world, and that nothing was created that wasn't created by Him. Picture it. All of the earth has been laid out. The beauty of the mountains, the power of the raging seas, the wonder of plant and animal life have all been placed on the wonderous earth that God has made. But there was more to be done. So, God turned to Jesus and said, *"Let us make man in our own image."* Grasp the depth of that conversation. God telling Jesus that man would fail, that the relationship between God and man would be broken, that Jesus would have to die in order for the relationship to be restored, and Jesus said, *"Let's do it."* Have you encountered *that* Jesus? The one who planned to die for you from the very beginning. The Jesus who was beaten, mocked, betrayed, and utterly humiliated for you. The Son who was separated from the Father by *your* sin. That's the Jesus that scripture is all about! And Isaiah got a taste of just what Jesus would bring, over 700 years before Jesus would even appear on earth.

As Isaiah looked upwards at his vision of God, he came face to face with just how broken he was. Hopefully; at this point, you have prayed over your own brokenness and experienced just how short you fall of God's standard. Understanding how broken you are makes up the difference between knowing who Jesus is, and having a desperation for the Son of God. As Isaiah stood, looking into the throne room of the Almighty God, he understood how sinful he was, and he admitted it before the Lord. Isaiah exclaimed his woe, and confessed his sin specifically, and audibly, before God. And what happens next is amazing, but in Isaiah's time, it would have been entirely unthinkable. Even as Isaiah stands there, an enemy of the Lord, one of the seraphim flies to him with a coal from the altar that is in the throne room,

"Then one of the seraphim flew to me, and in his hand was a glowing coal that he had taken from the altar with tongs. He touched my mouth with it and said: Now that this has touched your lips, your iniquity is removed, and your sin atoned for."

Imagine that! As he stands there, understanding fully that he deserves to die, one of the magnificent burning angels grabs a coal from the altar and flies towards Isaiah. I don't know about you, but I would be thinking, *"this is it."* A giant, burning angel is flying towards him with a glowing hot coal in a set of tongs, and Isaiah must have thought it was over. But the seraphim reaches out and touches Isaiah's *lips* with the coal, saying, *"Your iniquity is removed, and your sins atoned for."* In other words, the angel told Isaiah that it was finished. But don't miss the importance of the seraphim touching Isaiah's lips with the coal. It's specific! Isaiah specifically confessed his own filthy lips to God, and God provided specific forgiveness. That's what Jesus does. He didn't just die so that you could go to heaven, He rose again so that you could be made new! Paul tells us that any person who is in Christ Jesus is not only forgiven, but a new creation. Jesus longs to change you from the inside out, to make you whole, to purify you. And He did the work to do just that, 2,000 years ago on an old rugged cross. This is the Jesus that you need to develop a desperation for.

So where do you go to find Him?

The answer is back in John chapter 1, *"In the beginning was the word, and the word was with God, and the word was God…and the word became flesh and dwelt among men."* You begin to develop a desperation for Jesus Christ when you develop a desperation for His word. As I said earlier, the entirety of scripture is about Him. You have already seen that He was there in the beginning, but He remains all through the Old Testament. Remember, Jesus was never plan B! When Isaac had grown up a little bit God spoke to Abraham, asking him to sacrifice his own son. God tells Abraham, *"Take your son, your only son, whom you love,"* and he tells Abraham to sacrifice him as an atonement offering! It sounds insanc, and to a normal person it is, but God had a plan, and we Christians definitely aren't normal. God had a point to make to all of history. As Abraham raised the knife to kill his only son, *whom he loved*, God provided the replacement. The ram that the Lord provided was a picture of Christ all the way back in Genesis. The penalty for your sin is so much greater than even sacrificing your own child, *whom you love!*

But God always had a plan to provide the replacement. Jesus is the propitiation. But thank God Abraham's story isn't the only place we are painted a portrait of Jesus in the Old Testament. We know already that Isaiah's sin was atoned for because of the mercy of God, but so many more of the stories of old point to Jesus Christ. The great Exodus points to the covering of sin by the blood of the lamb. The

Israelites were to smear the blood of an unblemished lamb on their doorposts on the eve of the Passover, in order to spare their own first-born sons, and the wrath of God came upon every household that had not offered the sacrifice. As the angel of death passed through all of Egypt he would see the blood smeared over the doorpost as a sign that that household was to be spared from judgement. Can you fathom how desperate the Israelites must have been to get that blood over the door? They knew the wrath of God and the surety of every promise He made. They knew that, if they failed to apply the blood that they would certainly suffer. Isn't that a beautiful, and powerful picture of Jesus? I imagine that judgement day will be very much the same. As we stand before the great white throne of Judgement we will be examined and the penalty for conviction is death everlasting. The wailing of the Egyptians the morning after Passover will be nothing compared to the cries of agony in hell for all of eternity. But imagine as you stand there waiting to be judged, watching as people are cast into the lake of fire, and it's your turn to stand before the God of eternity. But He doesn't see your sin. He doesn't see your guilt or your shame. He doesn't see the wickedness that you are so painfully aware of. He only sees the blood of the lamb, and His judgement passes you by because the price of your iniquity has already been paid. Praise Jesus! That is the story of all who have given themselves over to a desperation for Jesus Christ. Your sin has been atoned for and the God of the universe sees only the blood of His perfect Son in you. Have you smeared the blood of the lamb over the doorpost of your life? Are you marked by the blood of the only perfect sacrifice? Will God see His son when He looks on you, or will He see only your wickedness? The blood has been provided, apply it!

As we have established, the grace of God, and the salvation that He would provide for the whole world, is a major theme throughout all of the Old Testament.

The Israelites were all given a glimpse of that salvation at the Passover, and David was a man who was very in tune with the salvation that only God would, one day, provide. Long before Jesus took on the flesh of man to take away the sin of the world David wrote of the coming salvation. *"How joyful is the one whose transgression is forgiven; whose sin is covered! How joyful is a person who the Lord does not charge with iniquity and in whose spirit is no deceit!"* In Psalm 32 David lays out two separate stories, a story of salvation and a story of continued brokenness. He creates a beautiful display of the difference between being forgiven and carrying the burden of sin. The way that you felt when you

examined yourself in the last chapter, that's exactly

what David claims it is like to hold on to his own sin.

He writes to God that, when he held on to his own sin

his bones became brittle, and God's hand was heavy

upon him. But praise Jesus, God took that sin away!

David felt salvation in a time when it was impossible

to experience the salvation that God would one day

bring. How? How could men like Isaiah and David

experience what God had not yet given for the world?

Because God was pointing to Jesus the entire time!

Do not allow your heart to miss the importance of

Jesus in all of scripture. It's all about the coming

salvation through Jesus Christ!

Many of the heroes we read about in the first half of the Bible were able to experience the salvation that God was promising through His own son. I could fill an entire book simply with the men and women who were able to catch a glimpse of salvation in the Old Testament. Hebrews 11 tells us that all of these men and women died in faith, having not seen the salvation that they were looking forward to, but knowing that God would provide it. But there is even more! Not only is the salvation from God foreshadowed all throughout the Old Testament, but the coming of Jesus is specifically prophesied

hundreds of years before He took on flesh. Psalm 22

lays out the life of Jesus from birth to brutal death. He

begins with the question, *"My God my God, why have*

you abandoned me?" This is what Christ cries out

from the cross in the moment that the sin of the world

separated the Son from the Father. And stew on that

for a second. In that moment, for the first time in all

of eternity, God and Jesus were separated by *your* sin.

For the very first time Jesus felt the despair of every

sinner, all at once. For the first time the Father turned

His back on the Son, and His heart was utterly

broken. All for you. And David wrote about that

moment hundreds of years before the birth of Christ.

David writes the first half of Psalm 22 from the perspective of Jesus Christ, though I don't believe he had any idea that that was that he was doing so. In verses 6-8 David writes, *But I am a worm and not a man, scorned by mankind and despised by people. Everyone who sees me mocks me, they sneer and shake their heads. "He relies on the Lord; Let him save him; let the Lord rescue him since he takes pleasure in him."* David describes, almost verbatim, what people did and said to Christ as He was crucified centuries after Psalm 22 was written. David even prophesies the crucifixion centuries before crucifixion was invented! That's insane. Crucifixion hadn't even been thought of yet in the time of David, and he writes, *"For dogs have surrounded me; a gang of evildoers has closed in on me; they pierced my hands and feet."* No other religion has this much fulfilled prophecy. And that's just one chapter, from one man! David wrote two other Psalms that we call "messianic" Psalms. And many other Psalms prophesy to the coming of Jesus. Psalm 8:2 prophesies that Jesus would be praised by the children. In Psalm 31:5 David exclaims, *"into your hands I entrust my spirit,"* The very words of Jesus in the moment that He handed His life over for the sins of the world. Psalm 69 foreshadows the gall and vinegar that was given to Christ on the cross. And the list goes on! Isaiah prophesies about the coming of Jesus 32 times! He is even specific enough to mention *"the voice crying out in the wilderness,"* Preparing the way of the Lord. That's John the Baptist! The coming of Jesus was planned far in advance, and it was planned to restore you! And so many more foretold the coming of Jesus. Ezekiel, Amos, Micah, Habakkuk, Zephaniah, all pointed to the coming of Jesus Christ. And He came! We hear so many predictions about our future today. Who will become the next president, when the world will end, who will win the next Super Bowl or World Series, but no one has the perfect track record that Bible lays claim to, because God knew. God, rich in mercy, planned to redeem you from the very beginning. And He did it through Jesus Christ.

So, where do you go from here? What do you do with this Jesus who wants to redeem and transform you? I guess the question that probably plagues you is this, *"can I really be transformed?"* You may not think it's possible. Even if you have been saved for years, you struggle with the idea that Jesus can change you, that He can make you holy. I struggle with it on a daily basis because, like Isaiah, I know who I am. And you know who you are. You know that your sinful nature continues to battle with the spirit of God that is in you, if you have accepted Jesus as your Lord and savior. And that is okay. I know you're not alone, because I often feel the same. It's called spiritual warfare, and you are not the first to feel like you are losing the battle. Paul, yes that Paul, the man who wrote the majority of the New Testament, struggled with the same feeling of self-loathing. *"For I know that nothing good lives in me, that is, in my flesh. For the desire to do what is good is with me, but there is no ability to do it. For I do not do the good that I want to do, but I practice the evil that I do not want to do.*" Paul, the man who fathered churches, ministered to the other apostles, rebuked those who were wrong, and encouraged those who were following after Jesus, felt like he could never win the war against his own sinful nature. And he couldn't! He admitted that there was nothing that he could do to overcome his own wickedness. He goes on to say, "*What a wretched man I am! Who will rescue me from this body of death? Thanks be to God through Jesus Christ our Lord! So then, with my mind I myself am serving the law of God, but with my flesh, the law of sin.*" That's right. Paul was desperate for Jesus, because he knew that there was no good within himself. And you need

to know that deeply, to know a desperation for Jesus

Christ. You need to know that Jesus Christ came to set

you free and transform your heart. And He will do it.

Jesus promised so many times, through His word, that

He can, and will, make you holy. Paul tells us that

Jesus, who begins to work in each of us the day that

we are saved, will continue doing His work until the

day it is completed, the day He returns for His

beloved. The day He returns for you. Peter calls each

one of us to be holy, as God is holy, and God does not

call His children to do things that He is unable to do

in them. Jesus Himself tells us that He is the vine, and

we are the branches. He promises that, if we remain in Him, He will remain in us, continuing His work in our hearts. But my personal favorite is found in Philippians chapter 2. *"For it is God who is working in you both to will and to work according to His good purpose."* Isn't that amazing? God not only works inside of you, but He gives you the *will* to live in holiness! It's not all on you. You don't have to carry the weight of your shortcomings on your shoulders, because God is constantly working inside of you. Praise God! Because you are weak, but in your weakness, He is made strong because Jesus Christ died and rose to make you holy. The answer is yes!

You can be holy. You can be transformed. Through the blood of Jesus, you can be made new. Live in that. Walk in that spirit by becoming desperate for Jesus Christ. Not only is it made possible for you to fall on your knees, humble yourself, and be renewed by Jesus Christ. It's what He desperately desires for you.

The key to becoming desperate for Jesus, is Jesus. When you come before God, fully aware of just how holy He is, and find yourself undone by your sinfulness, you will find yourself faced with a choice...desperation or denial. You can harden your heart and hold fast to your pride. David went through these moments, and it left him with brittle bones and

festering wounds until he humbled himself and laid

his wickedness before God. Or you can fall on your

face in desperation before Jesus, mourn over your

sinful nature, and run into the arms of the savior who

died to set you free.

Determine to be desperate for Jesus today.

[Please take a moment at this point in the book and

pray. If you have never accepted Jesus Christ as your

Lord and savior I praise God that you picked up a

copy of "Determined to be Desperate" and I urge you

to ask Jesus Christ to save you from your sin and

begin His transforming work within you today. If you have known Jesus Christ as your Lord, I hope that something has come to the forefront of your heart by now. I hope that you are fully aware of what it is within your heart that makes the heart of God sad, and the transforming work that Jesus wants to work within you today. Pray that Jesus Christ will make you desperate for Him, and I promise you He will.]

"THE OUWARD LOOK"

" "As a kid we would step out on those thick summer nights and collect lightening bugs. And with a mason jar chock full of them, their combined brilliance would light up my hands as I held them. But, if I released them from the jar, their brilliance would light up the world, which now included the hands of everyone around me. And as I think about the light of the Gospel and the utter brilliance of its message, as Christians maybe we should get rid of our jars."

* Craig D. Lounsbrough

You will never remain desperate for Jesus Christ if you fail to be desperate for the lost. When you accept Christ into your life to be your Lord and savior, you accept the greatest gift ever given to mankind. But you aren't the only person who needs that gift, and you are commanded to take it to those who still live without it. As a believer you are called to so much more than salvation, you are called to be a witness, and you will never remain desperate for Jesus if you refuse to be a witness. Remember the prayer of Isaiah when he stood face to face with the God of Armies? He not only confessed his own sin before the Lord, but the sin of those around him. So, after being blessed with atonement, Isaiah receives a call to be a witness to all that he has seen, and more.

"Then I heard the voice of the Lord saying:

Who should I send? Who will go for us?

I said: Here I am. Send me."

It is vital to notice that this wasn't a call specific to Isaiah. This was a call going out from the mouth of the Lord to anyone, it would seem, who was available and willing to go. And Isaiah volunteers before he even knows where he is going. Isn't that just like the Lord? He called Abram to go, without telling him where, or how far. He called each of the disciples without ever telling them all that they would face, and Paul had to go to a man to receive his sight before he was told what he was supposed to do with his new-found salvation. The Lord offers, to His witnesses, strength for today and hope for tomorrow, but so often you will not know much more than the call that is placed on you to be a witness. But you must answer that call. Go back to Isaiah and notice the call that he received. Isaiah was in the presence of God. He had seen the Lord of Lords. He had come to grips with how woefully awful the state of his heart was. And he had been offered the forgiveness of the full depths of his sin. *Then* he heard the voice of the Lord asking,

"Who should I send?" It is my hope that you are in that place now, the place that will allow you to discern that call that is always going forth for all believers, the call to go. If you are in that place, and your heart has been softened to the voice of the Lord, you should have a burning desire to reach the lost around you. Think about it. Do you remember when you were first saved? The fire that you had for the Lord. The need you had to tell people about what you had experienced. That is what Isaiah was experiencing. I was called to preach when I was 17 years old. I had little to no public speaking skills, in fact, I hated speaking in front of people. It made me

want to throw up, and it still does. But I remember

what it felt like when I was called to preach my first

sermon. I hadn't even written it out yet, but I had

something on my heart, and I *needed* to get it out. It

wasn't enough for me to simply study Christ as our

shepherd, trust me I tried. I had to say something.

And I truly believe that is the closest I have come to

hearing the call in the way that Isaiah did. But I don't

want you to think that call only comes to those who

are led to preach. The call can be a yearning to speak

to a certain person, or to tell a certain part of your

story. It can come as a person reaching out for help, or

an enemy who constantly seems to pick you out of a

crowd. It is the call to be a witness, and it is ever a part of your life if you have accepted Jesus Christ.

The final command that Jesus gave to His disciples, before ascending into heaven, was the call to be a witness.

"But you will receive power when the Holy spirit has come upon you and you will be my witnesses in Jerusalem, in all Judea and Samaria, and to the ends of the earth."

The call to witness was, quite literally, the very beginning of the church. And you are receiving that call now. So how do you respond to it?

How did Isaiah respond?

Take a look at his answer. There are two things that are vitally important for you to understand when you read the call, and answer, of Isaiah.

The first is his answer. Isaiah finds himself in the perfect spiritual position to hear the call of the Lord, and he answers, *"Here I am. Send me."* This isn't arrogance. Isaiah didn't point his nose up, grab the front of his coat, and yell out, *"hey! I'm it! I'm the right guy for the job."* That's not the attitude we see throughout Isaiah at all. I think that, in the most humbling moment of his life, Isaiah knew that he needed to answer that call, and he did so with the utmost humility. I picture the man, still unable to stand, raising his head just a little and saying, *"I'm here. Will I do?"* The answer to the call of the Lord must always come from a place of humility. Rich Mullins had one of my favorite quotes of all time, I have considered printing it off and hanging it in my office many times,

"God spoke to Balaam through his ass, and He has been speaking through asses ever since. So if God should choose to speak through you, you need not think too highly of yourself." – Rich Mullins

I love it! Because God so loves to use the broken and rejected in our world to testify to the greatness of His gospel. God is not in the business of finding the best and brightest to get His message across, He prefers to use people like you and me because, in our brokenness, He is glorified. Abram was afraid, and even gave away his own wife, calling her his sister, to try to stay alive. And then he even committed adultery to try to speed up the promise that God had made to him. Isaac played favorites with his own sons, and Jacob was a coward and a liar. The list could go on and on for an entire book, but the Bible is full of people who had no right to be used by God, who were used anyway. So, if the heroes of scripture had every reason to be humbled before the Lord, so do you. As you experience the call of the Lord to go and be a witness, don't let it become about you. It is so easy to allow the Lord's call on your life to become what *you* can do for *Him*, when it truly is all about what *He* loves you enough to do through *you*. Never lose the view of yourself that Paul had of himself, *"This saying is trustworthy and deserving of full acceptance: Christ Jesus came into the world to save sinners – and I am the worst of them."* You are the chief of sinners, leading other chiefs to the one who made you whole, the only hope that they have. You are a wretch leading other wretches to the only one who loves and transforms the worst of the worst. You are called to be a witness to the depth of your sin and those around you, and the abounding love of Jesus that has set you free. Commit to do so humbly and in awe of the one by whom you have been called.

The second thing I want you to see in Isaiah's answer to God's call for a witness is the nightmare that Isaiah was told he would endure. Isaiah was given a task that is a preacher's worst nightmare, to preach to a people who would never turn to the Lord. As soon as Isaiah calls out to the Lord, *"Here I am. Send me."*, God tells him to,

"Go and say to these people: keep listening but do

not understand; keep looking but do not perceive.

Dull the minds of these people; deafen their ears and

blind their eyes; otherwise they might see with their

eyes and hear with their ears, understand with their

minds, turn back, and be healed."

God sent Isaiah to a people who had been handed

over to the wickedness of their hearts and said, *"tell*

the truth." There were none who would listen. No one

would turn back to God for salvation because of the

words of Isaiah the prophet. But he was called to

proclaim the judgement and mercy of God anyway.

You need to know that looking outward is not about

numbers, but faithfulness. You must be faithful to the

word of God even if no one listens. We live in a culture, even amongst Christians, full of people who want to twist the gospel to make it more appealing. Isaiah could have preached a message of acceptance, tolerance, and the basic goodness of the Israelites, and I guarantee he would have had a massive following. He could have preached to the nation of Israel that God is a loving God, that He would overcome their enemies and lead them into prosperity, and Isaiah would have been the most popular prophet to have preached in the Old Testament. But that would not have been the whole truth that Isaiah was called to preach. It is true that God was, and is loving, but He is also just. And Isaiah was called to point to the justice of God and the judgement that was in store for the nation of Israel, as well as the depth of the mercy of God. Had Isaiah affirmed the innate goodness of man he would have gathered a large following, while walking away from the truth that God had called him to preach. Instead we find Isaiah telling the Israelites, (and us), that all of us have been led astray and even our good deeds are filthy without the mercy of God to make them clean. Otherwise there would have been no need for Christ to be pierced for our transgressions. The truth is, quite often, unpopular, because the truth is uncomfortable.

But the truth is all that the Lord will call you to be a witness to. Know that any voice that calls you to bear witness to a prosperity centered gospel is not the voice of the Lord, but the voice of the evil one. Yes, Satan calls out to you too. Satan wishes to lead you to bear witness to a false gospel. This is the reason that we have always seen heresy pop up in the church. The early church dealt with it (that's the reason for many of Paul's letters) and we deal with it in our churches today. Often these false gospels come from a desire to make the Bible look appealing to the world. We lean towards making others comfortable with a version of the truth, rather than making people uncomfortable with the sharp truth of the gospel. Be aware of this because it is prevalent, and it is not of God. The devil will call you to preach a gospel that accepts everyone but requires no change. The gospel of Jesus Christ accepts everyone and transforms all who would believe. The devil will call you to preach a gospel that doesn't include the terrible reality of hell. Jesus' gospel tells of the woes of hell, and the love of the savior who lives in heaven. As you begin to look outward be aware of the gospel you are preaching and know that, even if no one listens, the truth of the gospel is all that you must preach.

As you begin to take an outward look your story is vital to the spreading of the gospel. Your story is meant to be shared, and Jesus wants to show Himself to others through your experience, your salvation, and your journey home to where Jesus Christ has prepared a place for you. People need to hear about Jesus and you. People need to hear about what Jesus has done in, for, and through you. And people need to see Jesus in your life. You need to begin to develop a desperation for Jesus Christ that extends well past your life, to your Jerusalem, your Judea and Samaria, and the ends of the earth. You will find that, the more you become desperate for people to come to Jesus, the more desperate you will be to come to Jesus each and every day. Allow your heart to be broken for the lost and continue to convince yourself that the gospel is the one thing that the lost need most. Allow anyone who has ears to hear what Jesus has done in your life and what He so desperately desires to do in their lives. As you begin to train your heart to be desperate for the lost, pray. Pray that the Lord would make your heart tender. Pray that God would make you aware of every opportunity that you will have to share the gospel. Pray that God would place you in relationships with lost people so that you may have a kingdom impact in their hearts. And pray that God will ever continue to change you to look like Jesus,

share His gospel, and look outward as you walk the

Christian walk.

"DETERMINE TO BE DESPERATE"

"a man there was, though some did count him mad,

the more he cast away the more he had."

‾*John Bunyan, The Pilgrim's Progress*

This is the key to becoming desperate for Jesus.

Unless you divorce yourself, you will never develop a

deep-seated desperation for your Lord and savior.

Following Jesus Christ will cost you everything, to a

point where others who do not know Christ will call

you insane. Paul said that he counted all that he had

ever held dear as a loss. He even goes on to say that

he desires to share the sufferings of Jesus Christ and share in His death. That makes no sense to one who has never experienced the saving grace of Jesus Christ. It's madness to the world, but it is reality to those who have been saved. John the Baptist claimed that he *needed* to decrease as Christ increased. And he did. John the Baptist needed to get out of the way so that Jesus Christ could come in and do all that God had led John to testify about. John had to leave his own fame and glory behind, even to the point of losing his life for the sake of the gospel. In fact all of the disciples and many of the fathers of the early church lost everything in service to the gospel, up to their lives. Peter was crucified upside down because he refused to seek his own will but sought the will of God. Peter was so empty of himself by the time that he was martyred that he refused to be crucified in the same that that Christ was because he didn't even feel worthy to die in the same manner as his savior.

Andrew was crucified for the sake of the gospel. Thomas was pierced with spears by soldiers in modern day India. James was stoned *and then* clubbed to death. Matthias was burned to death. And so many more were hunted down and killed for the sake of the gospel. John was the only disciple who was not martyred for the sake of Christianity. Instead he was exiled to the Island of Patmos where the

second coming of Jesus was revealed to him by God.

The men who wrote the Bible and led the way in

establishing the early church were able to do so

because they had a habit of emptying themselves

before the Lord.

You need to do the same.

When the disciples asked Jesus who would be the

greatest in the kingdom of heaven the Lord did not

point to great and mighty leaders, or feats of

greatness, but to a child. Jesus told His disciples,

"unless you turn and become like one of these

children, you will never enter the kingdom of Heaven.

Therefore, whoever humbles himself like this child –

this one is the greatest in the kingdom of heaven."

Jesus desires you to come to Him in humility because

there is no other way to come to Him. You must come

to Jesus Christ, today and every day, broken and

empty of yourself. The reason the rich young ruler

walked away when Jesus told him to go and sell all he

had was because he was not desperate for the Lord,

but for salvation. See, it's possible to be desperate for

the blessings of God without being desperate for the

Son, and that will lead you not to the Lord, but to

walk away dejected and still utterly lost.

You need to be desperate for Jesus. You need to look

to God. Ask Him to show Himself to you. Stand and be amazed at the awesome wonder of the Lord. Allow Him to show you His majesty. Beg Him to reveal His might to you. Let Him show you how holy and unattainable He truly is. Take an upward look at the Lord of Armies and be amazed by Him.

You need to see the depths of your own sin. You have a deep need to see yourself for who you are, far from the Lord who desires to be your Father. On your own you fall brutally short of who you must be to walk with God. You need to see that you are broken and need to be fixed. You need to see that there is no amount of work that you can do to be made whole.

Look inside and see that you have deeply offended

the creator of this world, and your heart. Ask the Lord

to reveal to you the depths of your depravity, even if

you have been saved for years, you need to be

reminded that you fall short apart from Jesus. You

have a deep need to take an inward look, be appalled

by what you see, and turn to the only one who can

make you whole.

You need to look to Jesus. You need to see Him for

who He is, the lamb that was slain for the sin of the

world. You need to rest in the truth of the gospel, that

Christ came so that you may be saved and

transformed. You have a desperate need to see that

Jesus Christ bought your heart, and that you don't belong to yourself or to this world. You belong to Jesus Christ. You belong *with* Jesus Christ. You need the savior of this world who came, not to condemn the world, but that the world through Him might be saved.

And you need to see the lost. You have a need to see that the world around you desperately needs Jesus. You need to know that you will never remain desperate for Jesus if you are not desperate for the world to know Him, and Him crucified. You need to be confident in this, that those who have not accepted Christ on the day of reckoning will face eternity apart from God, in the depths of hell. You need to know

that people need Jesus. You need to take an outward

look at the world around you, lift up your face, pray,

and preach the truth of the gospel to all who need to

know that there is a savior who died, and rose again,

to set them free.

You need to be desperate for Jesus. You need to

determine in your heart today that you will seek first

His kingdom, humble yourself, and be His until the

day that He returns or takes you home.

Are you determined to be desperate?